HIP-HOP

Ashanti

Rosa Waters

Mason Crest Publishers

Ashanti

FRONTIS As a singer, writer, dancer, and actress, hip-hop star Ashanti is a
powerhouse in the arts.

PRODUCED BY 21ST CENTURY PUBLISHING AND COMMUNICATIONS, INC.

EDITORIAL BY HARDING HOUSE PUBLISHING SERVICES, INC.

MASON CREST PUBLISHERS INC.
370 Reed Road
Broomall, Pennsylvania 19008
(866)MCP-BOOK (toll free)
www.masoncrest.com

Printed in the U.S.A.

First Printing

9 8 7 6 5 4 3 2 1

Library of Congress Cataloging-in-Publication Data

Waters, Rosa.
   Ashanti / by Rosa Waters.
     p. cm. — (Hip-hop)
   Includes bibliographical references and index.
   Hardback edition: ISBN-13: 978-1-4222-0111-4
   Hardback edition: ISBN-10: 1-4222-0111-2
   Paperback edition: ISBN-13: 978-1-4222-0263-0
   1. Ashanti, 1980– —Juvenile literature. 2. Singers—United States—Biography—
Juvenile literature. I. Title. II. Series.
ML3930.A84W37 2007
782.421643092—dc22
[B]   2006010880

Publisher's notes:
- All quotations in this book come from original sources, and contain the spelling
  and grammatical inconsistencies of the original text.

- The Web sites mentioned in this book were active at the time of publication.
  The publisher is not responsible for Web sites that have changed their addresses
  or discontinued operation since the date of publication. The publisher will review
  and update the Web site addresses each time the book is reprinted.

Contents

Hip-Hop Timeline

1974 Hip-hop pioneer Afrika Bambaataa organizes the Universal Zulu Nation.

1988 *Yo! MTV Raps* premieres on MTV.

1970s Hip-hop as a cultural movement begins in the Bronx, New York City.

1985 *Krush Groove*, a hip-hop film about Def Jam Recordings, is released featuring Run-D.M.C., Kurtis Blow, LL Cool J, and the Beastie Boys.

1970s DJ Kool Herc pioneers the use of breaks, isolations, and repeats using two turntables.

1979 The Sugarhill Gang's song "Rapper's Delight" is the first hip-hop single to go gold.

1986 Run-D.M.C. are the first rappers to appear on the cover of *Rolling Stone* magazine.

1970   1980   1988

1976 Grandmaster Flash & the Furious Five pioneer hip-hop MCing and freestyle battles.

1986 Beastie Boys' album *Licensed to Ill* is released and becomes the best-selling rap album of the 1980s.

1970s Break dancing emerges at parties and in public places in New York City.

1982 Afrika Bambaataa embarks on the first European hip-hop tour.

1988 Hip-hop music annual record sales reaches $100 million.

1970s Graffiti artist Vic pioneers tagging on subway trains in New York City.

1984 *Graffiti Rock*, the first hip-hop television program, premieres.

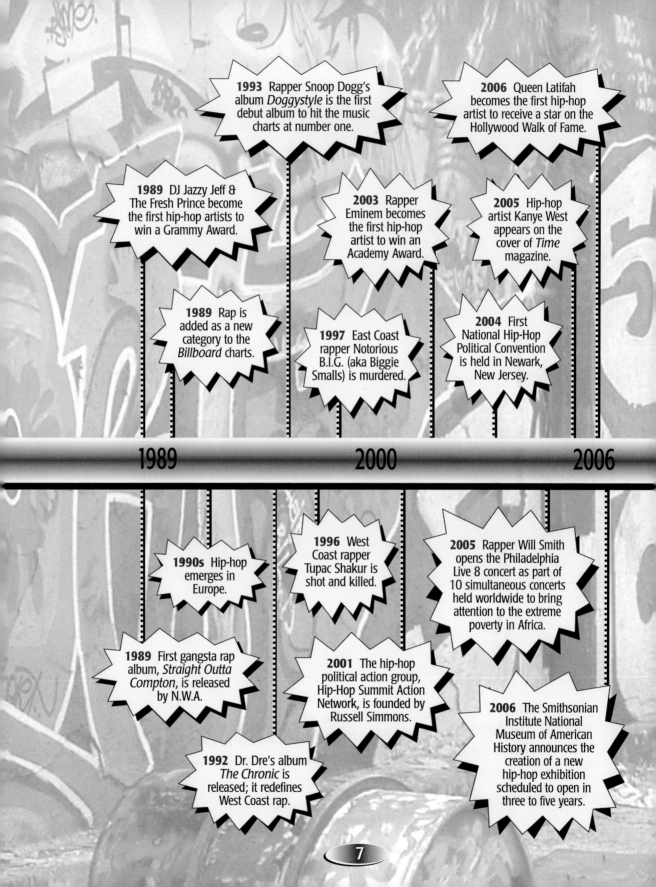

1993 Rapper Snoop Dogg's album *Doggystyle* is the first debut album to hit the music charts at number one.

2006 Queen Latifah becomes the first hip-hop artist to receive a star on the Hollywood Walk of Fame.

1989 DJ Jazzy Jeff & The Fresh Prince become the first hip-hop artists to win a Grammy Award.

2003 Rapper Eminem becomes the first hip-hop artist to win an Academy Award.

2005 Hip-hop artist Kanye West appears on the cover of *Time* magazine.

1989 Rap is added as a new category to the *Billboard* charts.

1997 East Coast rapper Notorious B.I.G. (aka Biggie Smalls) is murdered.

2004 First National Hip-Hop Political Convention is held in Newark, New Jersey.

1989   2000   2006

1990s Hip-hop emerges in Europe.

1996 West Coast rapper Tupac Shakur is shot and killed.

2005 Rapper Will Smith opens the Philadelphia Live 8 concert as part of 10 simultaneous concerts held worldwide to bring attention to the extreme poverty in Africa.

1989 First gangsta rap album, *Straight Outta Compton*, is released by N.W.A.

2001 The hip-hop political action group, Hip-Hop Summit Action Network, is founded by Russell Simmons.

2006 The Smithsonian Institute National Museum of American History announces the creation of a new hip-hop exhibition scheduled to open in three to five years.

1992 Dr. Dre's album *The Chronic* is released; it redefines West Coast rap.

Here, Ashanti holds just two of the eight awards she won at the 2002 Billboard Music Awards. Among them was the Female Artist of the Year Award, a major win for such a young star.

1

And the Winner Is . . .

She almost went to Princeton University on an athletic scholarship, but she chose her singing career instead. For Ashanti Shequoyia Douglas, the gamble paid off. In just a few years, she was number one on the charts and on top of the world. She went from being a high school track-and-field star to the "princess of hip-hop soul."

Perhaps she was destined for greatness from the beginning. After all, greatness is the meaning of her very name. Ashanti shares her name with the legendary Ashanti people of West Africa, a people descended from an ancient kingdom once famed for its power and wealth. Ashanti has already done her name proud, accomplishing a remarkable amount for someone so young. Although she is best known for her music, she is also a writer, dancer, and actress.

You wouldn't know it from the level of Ashanti's fame today, but just a few years ago, she was a complete unknown in the music world. In the past, she had been encouraged to pursue a career in pop music, but her heart was in hip-hop and R&B. Ashanti knew she was picking the most difficult realm of the music world for a young woman. But her idol, Mary J. Blige, had made it in this male-dominated music scene, and Ashanti believed one day she would as well.

Hip-Hop: From the Bronx to the World

The term hip-hop refers to an urban cultural movement defined by its music (called rap), art (called graffiti or tagging), and dance (called b-boying or break dancing). The movement began in the African American and Latino communities of the Bronx, New York, in the 1970s. Today, hip-hop culture is influential all over the world and can be seen not only in the now-popular music that defines it, but also in the fashion, language, and other cultural elements it has inspired.

Hip-hop music has two major elements: MCing and DJing. The DJ creates the music by isolating the beat portions (or breaks) of existing songs and playing them simultaneously to create a new sound. Traditionally, this is done using two turntables (a record on each turntable) and basic equipment, including a mixer, amplifier, and speakers.

While the DJ mixes, the MC raps, delivering beat-driven rhymes to engage the crowd. Often MCs engage in "battles" attempting to out-rap each other. Although not one of its defining elements, beatboxing, creating drum- and bass-like beats using only the human voice, is also part of hip-hop music. Beatboxing faded from prominence for many years, but it is currently enjoying a **renaissance** in urban music the world over.

Breaking Into the All-Boy's Club

Hip-hop may seem like an unlikely world for a young, female song-writer like Ashanti to find her voice. MCing, DJing, and beatboxing have traditionally been the exclusive realms of male artists. In fact, hip-hop music and culture often attracts **controversy** for its explicit sexual lyrics, which many people argue are disrespectful, **exploitative**, and degrading of women. Violence also features prominently in much hip-hop music, causing further controversy. Some people criticize hip-hop, saying its brand of sexuality and violence represents a **misogynistic** culture that encourages the **objectification** and oppression of women.

Whether hip-hop is dangerously **chauvinistic** is hotly debated. But one thing is certain: until recently, hip-hop music was usually not a place where female artists found fame or success. The woman credited with changing that is Mary J. Blige, the "queen of hip-hop soul."

Mary J. Blige's music is famous for **melding** rhythm and blues, also known as R&B, with hip-hop. She was not the first woman to

One of the major influences on Ashanti's career was hip-hop star Mary J. Blige. She was a pioneer in the male-dominated music genre, proving that women could be critical and commercial successes. This paved the way for other female singers, including Ashanti.

combine R&B with hip-hop, but Blige has arguably done so the most successfully. She expanded the **genre** and created musical possibilities that female and male artists alike have embraced. She has gained great respect in the industry, acting as a groundbreaker and inspiration for other female artists, Ashanti among them.

Taking the Music World by Storm

In 2002, Ashanti catapulted from being a nameless sideline song-stress to an instant music **diva** with the well-timed release of two **collaborative** songs and her first solo single. Her first hit was "Always on Time" with rapper Ja Rule; Ashanti sang the female vocals. Following immediately on that song's heels came Fat Joe's "What's Luv," also featuring Ashanti in the female vocals. With "Always on Time" climbing to number one on the U.S. *Billboard* Hot 100, and "What's Luv" tearing up the airwaves to number two, Ashanti made history. This previously unknown singer was now the first featured female artist to have songs simultaneously in the top two positions of the *Billboard* chart.

Her explosion onto the hip-hop scene generated huge waves in the music world and sparked an immediately loyal fan base. In response, Ashanti and her record label, Murder Inc., decided to move up the date for her **debut** album's release. Until this point, Ashanti had always appeared second-rung to another star, but now she was stepping out on her own, and her fans couldn't wait. On April 9, 2002, her album *Ashanti* was released, and it leapt onto the *Billboard* 200 album chart at number one. The album went **gold** in its very first week of sales, selling an astonishing half a million copies in just a number of days. They were the best first-week sales ever recorded for a debut female artist. Suddenly, Ashanti was everywhere. Her voice dominated the airwaves, her videos commanded television screens, and her image graced countless magazines.

Ashanti's self-titled debut album made history in another way as well. The first single released from the album was the song called "Foolish." As with everything "Ashanti" at the time, it was an instant hit. It entered the top 10 of the *Billboard* Hot 100, while "Always on Time" and "What's Luv" were still there. When that happened, Ashanti became only the second artist to have her first three chart entries be in the top ten at the same time. The only other artists to ever accomplish this feat were the Beatles.

Ashanti's first success was a 2002 duet with rap singer Ja Rule (shown here in a 2004 performance). When a duet with Fat Joe also hit the charts, Ashanti became the first female artist to have her two songs in the top two positions of the *Billboard* charts simultaneously.

The "Princess of Hip-Hop"

Ashanti's album sales continued steadily. By two months after its release, the album had gone double **platinum**, selling more than two million copies, and the single "Foolish" reigned at number one for ten weeks. Eventually, *Ashanti* would go triple platinum in the United States and platinum in the United Kingdom. The album has sold more than six million copies worldwide. Ashanti had always looked up to

With success as both a duet and solo artist, Ashanti's legion of fans dubbed her the "Princess of Hip-Hop." In 2003, she received another title—Grammy winner—with her award for Best Contemporary R&B Album.

Mary J. Blige, the queen of hip-hop soul, and now the world recognized Ashanti as following in the queen's footsteps. Her fans dubbed her hip-hop soul's princess.

With such astonishing success in so short a period of time, awards and **accolades** were soon to follow. In 2002, the year of her first album's release, Ashanti received two Lady of Soul awards, one Teen Choice award, two MOBO awards, and eight Billboard Music awards, including Female Artist of the Year and R&B/Hip-Hop Artist of the Year. In 2003, the awards kept coming. Among them were two American Music awards, two Soul Train awards, a Nickelodeon Kids Choice award, and an NAACP Image award. In the music world, however, the highest measure of an artist's success is the Grammy Awards. And when the 2003 Grammy Awards rolled around, Ashanti was nominated for five of the coveted prizes. She was nominated for Best New Artist, Best Contemporary R&B Album for her album *Ashanti*, Best Rap/Sung Collaboration for the hit "Always on Time" with Ja Rule, Best Rap/Sung Collaboration for the hit "What's Luv" with Fat Joe, and Best Female R&B Vocal Performance for the hit "Foolish." At the end of the night, she walked away as the winner of Best Contemporary R&B Album. There could be no doubt: Ashanti had arrived and she was here to stay.

Little Ashanti Douglas (center) had a comfortable childhood in Glen Cove, New York, with many friends. Her talent for dance would come early, when she was just three years old. Ashanti's musical talent would be discovered when she was older—twelve years old.

Early Life

From her earliest days, Ashanti's life was touched by the musical and performance arts that would lead her to fame. Both of Ashanti's parents were artistic. Her mother was a dance instructor, and her father loved to sing—and these gifts were passed on to the little girl who eventually would bring her music to millions of fans.

Ashanti was born on October 13, 1980, in Glen Cove, a small city on the beaches of Long Island, New York. Her parents made the most of what the city had to offer. With fewer than 30,000 people, Glen Cove was a well-off community with little crime. Its close proximity to New York City made Glen Cove an ideal place to raise children, yet still have access to all of the benefits of the big city.

Ashanti was a young girl when she began performing in front of audiences. But it wasn't singing that first brought her to the stage. Instead, she followed in her mother's footsteps and danced her way into the limelight. Ashanti was just three years old when she began dancing. She studied dance, including tap, ballet, and African dance, at the Bernice Johnson Cultural Arts Center in Queens, New York. She performed at world-famous venues like Harlem's Apollo Theater and Manhattan's Carnegie Hall. She also appeared as a dancer in *Polly*, a made-for-television musical by Disney.

An Unexpected Discovery

Although she began singing in a **gospel** choir at age six, as a young girl, Ashanti didn't think about being a singer. That passion was ignited a little later in life. In fact, no one, including Ashanti and her parents, even realized she had musical talent until she was twelve. Ashanti relates the tale of her "discovery" in interviews. In a discussion with journalist Matt Diehl, she described the event this way:

> **"Let me take you way back. I never really wanted to sing—when I found out I could, it was an accident. I was twelve years old, doing chores in my house. When we did chores, my mom was like, 'No TV, no radio—just do what I told you to do.' So one day I'm singing while I'm vacuuming, and all of a sudden she comes flying down the steps, screaming, 'I thought I told you not to listen to the radio!' And I was like, 'Mom, that wasn't the radio—that was me! I was singing!' I was actually singing Mary J. Blige's 'Reminisce.' She made me sing it over again, and then she got my dad, and I had to sing it for him, too. After that, they were like, 'OK, I think she has something here.'"**

There could be no mistaking it: Ashanti had a talent that could not be denied. Realizing the power of their daughter's voice, Ashanti's parents focused on helping her hone her skills. Her mother worked as her manager and booked Ashanti in numerous talent shows. As a young teenager, Ashanti split her time between schoolwork (she was an honor student), extracurricular activities, and performances. Talent shows became a big part of her life, and it was at some of these shows that music-industry insiders took notice of the young girl from Glen Cove.

Ashanti's parents were artistic and encouraged her to partici-pate in music, theater, and dance. Her entire family continues to support Ashanti in her career. Here, her parents and sister (far left) join Ashanti at the 2005 premiere of the film *Coach Carter*.

Only two years after Ashanti's vacuuming performance caught her parents' ears, she was signing her first record deal. Although the partnership did not yield an album, and Ashanti decided not to stay with the agency, working with the company was an important step in building a professional career.

Talented Teenage Years

Ashanti was only in high school, but she was already facing the adult pressures and decisions that come with pursuing a performing arts career. With studying, participating in school activities, performing, and recording, her days were more than full. Nevertheless, while she was still in her teens, Ashanti found time to do something that would become as important to her as singing: she found the time to write. Writing became a cornerstone of her life, and it would also become the cornerstone of her career. She wrote poetry and her own songs, and she continues to do so to this day.

Ashanti was just a teenager, but she had already shown herself to be a gifted dancer, gifted singer, and now a gifted writer. And yet she still had more talents to show before her high school years were complete, talents that could lead her life in an all new direction, if she chose to pursue them.

It turned out that Ashanti's physical abilities did not end on the dance floor. They extended to the athletic field as well. Ashanti was a great sprinter, and her high school's track-and-field team recruited her to run the 100- and 200-meter sprints. Once she was on the team, her coaches asked her to try another event as well, since most track-and-field athletes compete in three events. She tried her hand—or rather her feet—at the triple jump and surprised everyone by being even better in the triple-jump sandpit than on the race track. Triple jump became her top event, and universities took note of her talents.

Taking the Plunge

At seventeen, Ashanti was one of the few teenagers in the world who had both talent agents and sports scouts knocking at her door. By 1998, as high school was coming to a close, Ashanti knew she had to make the most important decision of her life: to pursue her education or her singing career.

Success in the music industry is very difficult to achieve, even for the world's most talented people. But singing and songwriting were Ashanti's passions. She knew many people would tell her to play it safe and get an education. But she also knew she couldn't listen. She had to follow her dream.

With her mother still acting as manager, Ashanti signed a deal with a new recording company. Fresh out of high school and brimming with

Ashanti's teen years were full with studying, school activities, performing, recording, and writing. She was a good student and a gifted athlete, competing in track and field. Ashanti was pursued by many prestigious universities, but decided to commit herself to a career in music.

big dreams, Ashanti moved to Atlanta. She moved in with her uncle and went to work trying to break into the music industry.

Like all teenagers, Ashanti faced difficult times and experienced highs and lows as she strove for independence. Similar to many people her age, she struggled between wanting to be on her own and wanting

Like many other girls her age, teenage Ashanti discovered love. She moved to Atlanta to further her career, however, leaving her boyfriend in New York. The pain and struggle of that relationship became the source for some of her poetry and lyrics.

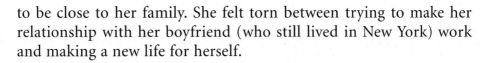

to be close to her family. She felt torn between trying to make her relationship with her boyfriend (who still lived in New York) work and making a new life for herself.

Life, Love, Struggle, and Determination

In her book, *Foolish/Unfoolish: Reflections on Love*, Ashanti recalls some of the emotional struggles she went through when she moved to Atlanta to pursue her singing career. She was supposed to be focusing on breaking into the music industry, but she was also just out of high school, young, and in love. She states, "I used to do lots of crazy things for love."

Like many people in love, Ashanti spent hours on the phone with her boyfriend. Sometimes she would want to see her boyfriend so badly that she would fly to New York to stay with him. She would even call her parents, pretend she was still in Atlanta, and say she was flying into New York to see them in a few days. A few days later, she would leave her boyfriend's house, go to her parents, and pretend she'd just arrived from Atlanta.

With the pressures of the long distance between them and Ashanti's singing career, the relationship ultimately didn't work out. The drama and emotional turmoil of that period took its toll and affected Ashanti's work. To make matters worse, Ashanti's relationship with the record company with which she had signed wasn't producing as she had hoped it would. Eventually, she severed the relationship. She got some minor film roles, making appearances in *Who's Da Man* and Spike Lee's *Malcolm X*, but musically, she had no big breaks. Disheartened but still determined, Ashanti packed up and returned to New York.

In 2000, back in New York, Ashanti signed with Murder Inc. Records. Her career was off and running, first as a backup singer for some of the major hip-hop artists of the day and then as a solo act.

3

Arriving at the Top

Back home in New York, surrounded by her supportive family, Ashanti continued singing, writing, working, and looking for that magic opportunity that would make her a success. Then, in 2000, producer Irv Gotti, one of the heads of Murder Inc. Records, noticed Ashanti. Everything was about to change in Ashanti's life.

When the opportunity to sign with Murder Inc. came, Ashanti wasn't immediately sure she should seize it. After all, would it be good "PR" to always have her name associated with the word "murder?" But Murder Inc. already successfully represented a number of big-name male rap stars, and the studio felt that bringing someone on board who was feminine and soulful would round out the company's talent. Ashanti's voice, looks, and **demeanor** fit the bill, and eventually both parties agreed the partnership was a good match. In 2001, under Gotti

Ashanti has sung backup for many of hip-hop's biggest names. In 2001, she posed with two of them—Vita (right) and Ja Rule—at *Teen People*'s party for its "What's Next" issue. She was also gaining notice as a songwriter.

and Murder Inc.'s **tutelage**, Ashanti began singing backup for some of the music industry's biggest stars.

No one knew her name yet, but Ashanti's voice was finally on the airwaves. In 2001, she sang background in Vita's "Justify My Love," a hip-hop remix of the song originally sung by Madonna; Big Pun's "How We Roll," one of many songs released after his death; and "I'm Real (Murder Remix)," a Jennifer Lopez song featuring Ja Rule.

Hitting the Big Time

Singing backup may not seem like a huge career move, but it was an important stepping-stone for Ashanti. The background work gave Ashanti the opportunity to get noticed, make contacts, gain experience, and develop relationships with her new label and colleagues.

Ashanti's talent as a songwriter also began grabbing attention and allowed her to collaborate on some big projects. One of the most important songs she worked on at this time was Jennifer Lopez's number-one single "Ain't It Funny," which Ashanti cowrote. As the months passed, Ashanti's projects became bigger and more meaningful. By the end of the year, with Murder Inc.'s experience and marketing behind her, Ashanti would be transformed from a nameless background singer into a rising star.

Ashanti made her first mark as a solo artist in 2002 with her album *Ashanti*. Here, she is ready to autograph copies of her CD for fans at Macy's in Herald Square, New York City.

The very next year, her collaborative works "Always on Time" and "What's Luv" and her single "Foolish" were constantly on the airwaves. It seemed like nothing could go wrong for Ashanti. The next single released from the *Ashanti* album, "Happy," reached the top 10. After that came the single "Baby," which made *Billboard*'s top 20, still a highly respectable showing. In 2002, *Ashanti* was the seventh-highest-selling album of the year, making the singer Murder Inc.'s top-selling artist. In an interview with *Billboard*, producer Irv Gotti described Ashanti's success: "She had flow, bounce, and content. There's no other artist that you can say has this much hip-hop urgency, but yet is R&B."

A good deal of Ashanti's success had to be credited to her abilities as a songwriter. The fact that she writes all her own songs makes Ashanti somewhat unique in the music industry, an industry where many artists have great voices and performance abilities but must rely on others to write their lyrics. In a 2003 article for *Ebony*, Ashanti was quoted regarding her songwriting. She stated:

> **"I feel it's definitely more passionate when they're your own words, when it comes from singing about reality, your emotions, your surroundings, your environment. My music has a touch of reality that everyone can relate to, whether they're old or young, Black or White."**

Ashanti Act Two

In the wake of her sudden musical fame, Ashanti decided to try her hand at another form of writing. In 2002, she published *Foolish/Unfoolish: Reflections on Love.* The book is a collection of poetry and essays exploring issues of love, relationships, and heartbreak. Most of the poems were written when Ashanti was a teenager. The poems are accompanied by explanations of what was happening in Ashanti's life at the time and the events and people that inspired her to write the poems. For many of Ashanti's fans, the book is an opportunity to get to know her better and to see the emotional life of "Ashanti the teenage girl in love."

With an album selling millions of copies and a new book, Ashanti could have chosen to take some time to sit back and simply enjoy her success. Her debut album had brought her fame, and she was raking in the awards. Nevertheless, she went hard to work on new projects and her next album.

FOOLISH/UNFOOLISH
Reflections on Love

Ashanti

In 2002, Ashanti also broke into the publishing world with her book, *Foolish/Unfoolish: Reflections on Love*. Filled with poetry and essays, most written while she was a teenager, the book offers experiences to which many readers can relate.

After their first successful collaboration, Ashanti decided to pair again with rapper Ja Rule. In 2003, they returned to the airwaves together with the hit "Mesmerize." Ashanti followed up by releasing her second album, *Chapter II*, which knocked *Dangerously in Love* by Beyoncé Knowles out of the number-one spot on the *Billboard* 200 album chart.

Chapter II was a successful follow-up to Ashanti's debut album, going platinum in the United States, gold in the United Kingdom, and selling over three million copies worldwide. The album's first single "Rock Wit You (Awww Baby)" hit number two on the Hot 100 chart. The single "Rain on Me" also made the top 10. The album brought another round of nominations and awards. Ashanti received Grammy nominations for Best Female R&B Vocal Performance for "Rain On Me," Best R&B Song for "Rock Wit U (Awww Baby)," and Best Contemporary R&B Album for *Chapter II*.

Ashanti Round Three

Ashanti began 2004 with yet another round of collaborations. She again partnered with Ja Rule on the single "Wonderful," which also featured R. Kelly. The single reached number five on the Hot 100 chart. Her collaboration with Lloyd on the single "Southside" earned a top-20 rating. Her single with Shyne, "Jimmy Choo," was not particularly successful, but its video was extremely popular.

At the end of the year, Ashanti released yet another album, *Concrete Rose*. It wasn't as big of a success as her previous two albums, but it still entered the *Billboard* 200 at number seven and went platinum in the United States, gold in the United Kingdom, and sold almost two million copies worldwide. The album's top single, "Only U," only reached number thirteen on the Hot 100 chart, but it peaked at number two in the United Kingdom. Its success overseas made "Only U" Ashanti's most popular song in the United Kingdom. Her third album generated enough sales to keep Ashanti rated as her label's top-selling artist three years in a row.

The success of *Ashanti*, *Chapter II*, and *Concrete Rose* generated other opportunities for the young, brightly burning star. Not only was she able to publish her own book of poetry, she also began making television appearances and receiving offers for product endorsements and movie roles. For the first few years of her career, Ashanti was hesitant to take on anything too hefty in the acting department for fear

Ashanti performs at a launch party for her album *Chapter II*. The rising star didn't suffer a sophomore jinx with her second CD. *Chapter II* went platinum and sold more than three million copies worldwide. It also brought her three Grammy nominations.

Successful with her music and her book, Ashanti became a frequent sight on television. Here she is shown performing on a 2003 telecast of the *Today Show*. She also spread her acting wings on shows such as *Sabrina*, *American Dreams*, and *Buffy the Vampire Slayer*.

it would compromise her focus on her singing career. She did make some small appearances, however. In 2002, she appeared on *American Dreams* and *Sabrina, the Teenage Witch*. In 2003, she made a guest appearance on *Buffy the Vampire Slayer*. And in 2004, she "got punk'd" by Ashton Kutcher for his hit show *Punk'd*. Also in 2004, Ashanti sang in Hindi for the **Bollywood** movie *Bride and Prejudice*.

All Is Not as It Seems

She was the princess of hip-hop soul, a Grammy Award winner, and an instant star. After her initial success, it may have seemed like life was going to be perfect and fame a smooth ride for Ashanti. But things are often not precisely as they seem.

It's true that 2002 was an incredible year for the young star. She reports in several interviews that back at the beginning of her career, when she heard one of her songs come onto the radio, she would sometimes jump out of her car and start leaping up and down in the street for joy. But the giddy happiness of those first months on the charts would soon be dulled by a few doses of some of the harsher sides of fame and the music industry.

VIBE

www.vibe.com

ASHANTI
LOVE ME OR LEAVE ME ALONE

AL GREEN
Hot grits and a tragic death

EAST COAST RAP
Who cares?

PLUS
EMINEM
TEGO CALDERÓN
ROSARIO DAWSON
ANITA BAKER
LIL SCRAPPY

U.S. $3.99/CAR $5.50 DECEMBER 2004

Though loved by her fans, Ashanti was often criticized by reviewers. Sometimes, they were downright cruel. In the cover story for the December issue of *VIBE*, she addresses that issue and the downside of fame.

4

Faltering Fame

Many in the music industry admired Ashanti's career. But although she loves her music, her job, her fans, and her success, she can also tell you that fame has a darker side. Unfortunately, Ashanti began to experience this darker side soon after her first album catapulted her into fans' hearts.

Ashanti's fame has brought her some of the typical trials experienced by well-known people. She has lost the freedom to go anywhere she wants any time she wants, the way other people do. She must always be accompanied by security to protect her from the mobs of people that can form if she is spotted. She also must endure the media's constant invasions into her privacy. As a music star, it's impossible for her to do just about anything, from visiting with family to going out on a date, without somebody publishing an article and speculating on the situation.

The need for security, loss of **anonymity**, and constant media scrutiny, however, are the typical prices people pay for fame. And many people in Ashanti's position say that although they wish they could have more freedom and privacy, they realize it's the tradeoff they make for their success. Ashanti probably feels the same way, but her negative experiences with fame have not ended with the typical daily trials.

Just a Pretty Face?

Almost as soon as Ashanti began experiencing success, she also began receiving criticism. Although many fans supported her, there were also people ready to pick apart her talent—or as they claimed, her lack thereof. Some music critics claimed she couldn't really sing; that her studio albums were fine, but her live performances revealed a weak voice and bland stage presence. Other critics claimed she was just a pretty face riding the coattails of more-talented male rappers.

People also compared Ashanti to other female hip-hop and R&B artists, saying that her abilities paled in comparison to performers like Mary J. Blige, Mariah Carey, Beyoncé, Alicia Keys, and others. They claimed Ashanti didn't have the soul of Blige, the voice of Carey, or the performance abilities of Beyoncé. Ashanti, they declared, was simply **mediocre**.

Critics began to commonly refer to Ashanti as a "soubrette," a term that comes originally from classical music but that is now used in popular music to describe a female singer with a pleasant, youthful, but limited voice. In popular music, the term is often cast in a less-than-complimentary fashion to describe a female singer whose best qualities are her youthful looks and personality, and whose voice needs the help of the studio to make it album-worthy.

Thus far, Ashanti's collaborations and albums have done little to dispel the rumors that she lacks any remarkable vocal ability. For the most part, her vocals both in duets and solo work are performed in the easily sung lower and middle ranges of her voice. People who have heard Ashanti's work from before she achieved fame, however, say that Ashanti's limited used of her **vocal register** did not begin until she signed with Murder Inc. They claim the vocal range she has shown of late has much more to do with decisions made in the studio and by Ashanti's management than with the singer's actual abilities.

An Anti-Ashanti Movement

Questions concerning her talent, however, haven't been the only negative reactions to Ashanti's success. Her first album brought her many

Some critics questioned Ashanti's singing ability. Could she *really* sing, or was she simply a studio phenomenon created through clever editing, mixing, and other technological tools? Ashanti continued her live performances to prove them wrong—and please her millions of fans.

fans and sparked nominations, awards, and fame. But all the positive buzz about her music also triggered a type of "anti-Ashanti" movement.

The fuss began after it was announced that the 2002 *Soul Train* awards intended to bestow on Ashanti the honor of Aretha Franklin Entertainer of the Year. That announcement got some people talking.

In 2002, Ashanti received the Aretha Franklin Entertainer of the Year Award from the *Soul Train* Lady of Soul Awards. Some people felt she didn't deserve the award and were very vocal in their opposition. But *Soul Train* stood by its decision, and by Ashanti.

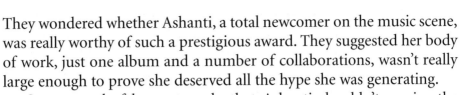

They wondered whether Ashanti, a total newcomer on the music scene, was really worthy of such a prestigious award. They suggested her body of work, just one album and a number of collaborations, wasn't really large enough to prove she deserved all the hype she was generating.

Some people felt so strongly that Ashanti shouldn't receive the honor that they decided to fight to have the award withdrawn. A high school student in California, Rommel Zamora, set the movement in motion when he created an online petition called "Better Candidate for the Aretha Franklin Award." The petition to *Soul Train* reads:

> **"We, the undersigned, feel that there are many superior entertainers that are more worthy of this award than Ashanti. It is an insult to other entertainers who are more deserving of the award and Aretha Franklin. Ashanti simply lacks singing ability and stage presence. She doesn't demonstrate the qualities of an entertainer and hasn't been out in the public for a full year. Better candidates for this award should be Faith Evans, Alicia Keys, India.Arie, or Aaliyah."**

In the weeks prior to the award, the petition collected thousands of signatures. It continues to be hosted and collect signatures on www.petitiononline.com and has been signed by over thirty thousand people. But the petition did not stop the award from going forward. *Soul Train* stood by the decision and came to Ashanti's defense, pointing out that, although she'd only been known to the public for a number of months, she had spent the better part of a decade working tirelessly to achieve her position and was more than deserving of the honor. The petition also sparked a number of online counter-petitions supporting *Soul Train*'s decision to honor Ashanti with the award.

Bad Rap for Murder Inc.

Ashanti's woes did not end with her critics. After 2002, her career was affected by difficulties at Murder Inc. as well. She had originally been hesitant to sign with the company that had the word "murder" featured so prominently in its name. Now the name was bringing trouble to the company and the artists it represented.

Producer Irv Gotti insisted the label's name had nothing to do with homicide. He and star Ja Rule explained in interviews that the name came from their habit of exuberantly declaring "It's murder!" when they finished or "killed" a track or achieved success. Nevertheless, some record stores didn't want to carry anything that had the label's name prominently displayed, and some fans and critics continued to be opposed to the use of the term "murder." There was speculation that "murder" was affecting *Chapter II* and other albums' sales. The controversy also made it difficult for Murder Inc. artists to get product endorsements.

To make matters worse, in January 2003, the FBI raided Murder Inc.'s offices, looking for a criminal connection between the label and Irv Gotti's friend, convicted drug offender, Kenneth McGriff, better known in the hip-hop world as "Supreme." The investigation grew to include the FBI; the Bureau of Alcohol, Tobacco, Firearms, and Explosives; the IRS; the New York City and Baltimore police departments; and others. The label, its artists, and its investors were clearly shaken. Later that year, Irv Gotti dropped "Murder" from the company's name, although he would not comment on whether the decision had anything to do with the negative publicity or the FBI raid. The company is now simply called The Inc.

Irv Gotti Arrested

In January 2005, Irv Gotti's troubles became much more serious. He and his brother, Chris Gotti, were arrested on **money-laundering** charges. After completing its investigation, the FBI believed the Gotti brothers had funneled more than one million dollars of McGriff's drug money through the record company. A number of other people associated with The Inc. and its artists were arrested on various similar charges.

After his hearing, Irv Gotti stated to the media:

> **"I want to make it very crystal clear that I don't look [badly] at the government in any way, shape, or form for them thinking I'm doing anything wrong. I call myself Gotti, I made my label Murder Inc., I grew up poor, from the street. But I don't look bad at them for thinking ill things of me. In no way have I done anything wrong except make great music that people seem to love. That's all I'm guilty of."**

Ashanti and her label-mates stood by Gotti throughout the trial, and she, Ja Rule, Jay-Z, and Fat Joe were in front-row seats during the

With hip-hop's reputation for violence, was Murder Inc. really such a good name for a record company? Although executives denied any connection with crime, in 2002, Ashanti, Irv Gotti, and Ja Rule announced that "murder" would be dropped from the company name, becoming The Inc.

closing arguments. In December 2005, the jury's verdict was handed down: Irv Gotti and his brother were cleared of all charges.

Career Stall or Freefall?

As the Gottis and The Inc. struggled with their legal woes, Ashanti was experiencing a court battle of her own. A contract she signed as a teenager came back to haunt her. Producer Genard Parker of T.E.A.M. Entertainment claimed Ashanti **breached** her contract and owed him millions of dollars, mostly in **royalties**. He claimed that he had helped the singer achieve her fame, that she dropped him the minute that fame was in sight, and that she failed to give him the compensation she had promised when they cut a deal to dissolve her contract. Ashanti

For Ashanti, along with fame came legal problems. Her first producer, who signed her as a teenager, claimed that since he helped her earn that fame, she owed him money. A jury agreed, and in 2005, she was forced to pay him more than $600,000.

fought the charges in court, but in July 2005, a jury ordered her to pay Parker $630,000.

Her legal troubles weren't the only ill effects Ashanti was suffering from her singing career. She was now plagued by a physical ailment as well. Her feet were in constant pain—and it turned out the cause of her discomfort was high fashion. Stars are always aware of needing to look good for the camera, and for Ashanti, an important part of "the look" is her shoes, usually pointy, high-heeled ones. But those shoes caused two of the bones in her feet to grow incorrectly, and the extremely painful ailment required surgery to correct.

Probably the worst of Ashanti's difficulties, however, was her album sales. Though all three of her albums went platinum, each sold fewer than the last. She had also released what some considered an ill-advised Christmas album, *Ashanti's Christmas*, in 2003 that sold barely over 100,000 copies. In 2005, she produced a collection of collaborations and remixes called *Collectables by Ashanti* that fared little better than the Christmas album and received some very negative reviews.

Ashanti had now gone nearly two years without a really big hit. Critics said her career had stalled; others claimed it was in total freefall. But Ashanti wasn't ready to give up.

Though Ashanti has achieved success tinged by a dose of difficulty, she goes onward, refusing to dwell on the bad things. She's recording new albums, building her acting career, and focusing on the good things—like looking glamorous at the Grammy Awards in February 2004.

◄ 5 ►

Ashanti Takes Control

Despite the criticism and difficulties, Ashanti is hard at work on her next album. She clearly plans on maintaining her diva status. For many fans and critics, this will be a make or break record. But Ashanti tries not to focus on the pressure. Instead, she's concentrating on the positives in her life and the opportunities fame has brought her.

In the last few years, Ashanti has had to learn who her friends are, and who they aren't. In interviews, she says she's cut those people who weren't true friends out of her life. And she stays positive with the help of all the wonderful fans, family, and friends who support her. She describes her current situation this way:

"I feel like a very blessed person. I have a lot of people that love me, and I'm surrounded by great, genuine people that help me, and we all work hard. It's taken such a long time to get here, so we're just very happy that it's working out the way it is."

While Ashanti is putting pen to paper creating new songs that she hopes will be hits, she's also beginning writing for what she hopes will be her second book. This book, she says, will be focused on the "behind-the-scenes" action of her life and the music industry in general. It's a topic her fans always want to learn more about. She is also thinking about writing a children's book or something else that would reach and inspire her very youngest fans. That project, however, may be further in the future.

From the Stage to the Big Screen

One of the high points in Ashanti's life right now is acting. She had done a number of very small appearances on television shows and in movies in the past, but in 2005, she made her true acting debut in the blockbuster movie *Coach Carter*, starring Samuel L. Jackson. Ashanti played the role of Kira, the pregnant, teenage girlfriend of a high school basketball star. She said she loved the role because it was true to life and showed some of the very serious adult issues that teenagers must sometimes face. *Coach Carter* opened at number one at the box office.

In 2005, Ashanti also starred in the made-for-television movie *The Muppets' Wizard of Oz*, a modern-day retelling of the famous original. In the movie, Ashanti played Dorothy Gale, an aspiring singer who leaves her Kansas trailer park in hopes of becoming a star.

In her third film role, Ashanti played a jealous girlfriend in *John Tucker Must Die*. The 2006 comedy is about three high school girls who find out they all have the same boyfriend. The girls clash over "their man" at first but then realize the true villain is the cheating boyfriend— so they plan revenge. Ashanti says that although the film's title and premise sound dark, it was really a lot of fun to make.

Ashanti also had fun filming a DVD that will give fans a peek into the backstage realities of her performing life. She says it offers a humorous side, revealing some of what can go wrong during live performances.

In 2005, Ashanti made her big-screen debut as a pregnant teenager (shown here in a scene with actor Rob Brown) in *Coach Carter*, starring Samuel L. Jackson. The film was successful, opening at the box office in the number-one slot. Ashanti hopes this is just the first of many more movie opportunities for her.

The Sweet Smell of Success

Fame has brought Ashanti opportunities beyond the performing arts world as well, and she has seized them with enthusiasm. One of her most recent projects was the creation of her own perfume. The perfume is called Precious Jewel and is sold at WalMart. When it launched, Ashanti remarked in an interview, "This project was very precious to me. I wanted everything to be perfect! I must've driven the fragrance developers nuts by making sure everything was exactly how I envisioned."

As if singing, acting, and writing were not enough, Ashanti has entered the fragrance world. In 2005, she introduced Precious Jewel to the world, a perfume she had worked on very hard, making sure it was exactly what she wanted.

Ashanti has also lent her image to a line of moderately priced jeans called Delicious Curves. The jeans are produced by Mudd and sold at Sears. They feature embellishments and detailing and are designed for curvier figures. Ashanti says she likes being a spokesperson for a product made for real bodies and affordable to real girls.

The hip-hop diva has a number of other product endorsements. One of them is Herbal Essences. The hair products even make an appearance in a shower scene in one of Ashanti's videos. Of seeing the Herbal Essences ad for the first time, Ashanti told *Ebony* magazine, "When I saw it, . . . I was so excited because I'm the first African American female to lead a national campaign for the product. It's an exciting feeling."

Fighting Back

In addition to taking control of her opportunities in music and film and capitalizing on her image, Ashanti is also fighting back against Genard Parker and T.E.A.M. Entertainment, who successfully sued her in 2005.

The year of their lawsuit, T.E.A.M. Entertainment released a compilation album called *Can't Stop*. It contained songs that Ashanti had recorded when she was sixteen. She claims she never gave permission for the songs to be released and that T.E.A.M. had no right to air the tracks after her contract with them was ended. She was further angered by the fact that the company used her picture and name on the album cover.

In February 2006, Ashanti began a lawsuit against Parker and his company. She is suing to have sales of the album stopped and over one million dollars paid to her in damages and lost profits.

But Ashanti isn't only focusing on the negative aspects of fame. She's also taking advantage of all the opportunities it gives her to do good in the world.

Despite the problems that have come with fame, Ashanti prefers to concentrate on the positives of being well known. One of them is the chance to give back and to make a difference in others' lives, such as through the *Today Show*'s Annual Toy Drive.

6

Dreams for a Better World

Many celebrities say that the greatest thing about achieving fame and fortune is that their success makes them influential with the public and brings them close to powerful people, thus putting them in a position to help others. Ashanti is no exception. On numerous occasions she has seized the opportunity to use her talents to help other people.

Many times Ashanti has used her voice, her image, and her celebrity to help support a cause. Whether it's fighting domestic violence, coming to the aid of needy children, or raising awareness about the AIDS crisis in Africa, Ashanti recognizes how strong an influence she can have with her fans, and that she can use that influence to make a difference in the world.

Performing for the Cause

Like many musicians, Ashanti often performs at events or participates in concerts to help raise money for worthy causes. In November 2002, Ashanti performed at the Neil Bogart Memorial Fund's Annual Tour for a Cure at the Universal Ampitheatre in Universal City, California. Named for record producer Neil Bogart, who died of cancer at age thirty-nine, the tour benefits the Neil Bogart Pediatric Cancer Research Program at Children's Hospital Los Angeles and other forms of cancer research. The 2002 tour was opened by Dick Clark and featured celebrities that included Ashanti, Britney Spears, and Sugar Ray.

Another benefit concert Ashanti took part in was the VH1 Save the Music Foundation's 2003 concert, which was titled "VH1 Divas Duets," at MGM Grand Garden Arena in Las Vegas, Nevada. The foundation works to restore instrumental music education programs in America's schools, programs that in recent years have been slashed around the country because of financial struggles in school systems. The foundation believes that music is an essential part of all children's education, and it also works to raise awareness around the country about music's importance in young people's lives and mental growth. Ashanti performed the song "Do I Do" with Stevie Wonder at the concert's finale.

In January 2004, Ashanti even went all the way to Nigeria, Africa, to perform in a concert called the "Battle of Hope." The concert was organized by Women Trafficking and Child Labour Education Foundation and was meant to raise awareness about AIDS in Africa, as well as spread the terrible stories of women and children being trafficked for sexual and slave labor.

Ashanti's singing isn't the only talent she can use to help a good cause. In 2005, she was in Hollywood, Florida, helping to conduct a hip-hop dance workshop to benefit the Hurricane Relief Fund. Ashanti, however, does not always even need to perform in order to help a cause. Just her mere presence can bring aid to those in need. For example, early in September 2005, she took part in the Fashion Rocks event held at Radio City Music Hall in New York City to benefit the victims of Hurricane Katrina. Just a few days later she was at a benefit for the American Cancer Society, the annual DreamBall, at the Waldorf Astoria in Manhattan. Later that same year, in December, she appeared at the *Today Show*'s Annual Toy Drive in New York City to help collect toys for needy children.

Another project Ashanti feels strongly about is VH1's Save the Music Foundation. In 2003, she performed a duet with Stevie Wonder for the "VH1 Divas Duets" concert. Proceeds went to benefit the foundation that helps keep instrumental music in the schools.

Fighting domestic violence is one of Ashanti's passions. She partnered with the Family Violence Prevention Fund to raise awareness about domestic abuse. In many of her interviews, she speaks out against domestic violence; she helped create public service announcements on domestic violence that have aired in more than four thousand movie theaters around America. On top of all that, she created a mini-movie with LidRock, with proceeds going to help stop domestic violence.

Ashanti's career has seen ups and downs, awards and criticisms. No one knows what will happen next, but everyone can be sure that Ashanti will take whatever comes in stride. She's in control of her life and her career.

Where to From Here?

Ashanti has sold millions of albums, served as the face of Mudd Jeans, and even managed to appear in a few movies in her spare time. She's made lots of money and experienced both the highs and lows of fame. Meanwhile, she's done her best to speak out on behalf of those in life who need some extra help.

And now she's ready for whatever comes next. She told Teen-Hollywood.com that she's currently in the studio working on her next album: "It's been really rough this year, but I think nothing can stop us. Me, Ja [Rule] and Irv [Gotti], we're in the studio recording music for our next album. . . . Some of the songs are so hot. . . ."

In February 2006, Ashanti revealed that she has plenty of ideas for the future—and not all of them have to do with music. At a dinner hosted by Miss Sixty to celebrate its New York runway debut, Ashanti said she is launching OPC Beauty Blend multivitamins in Miami. "I travel everywhere with my stylist and she's always getting sick, so I tell her to take her vitamins," Ashanti said. "She's not here tonight, in fact, because she's sick."

In interviews, when Ashanti is asked what advice she would give to other young people who are searching to find their way in life, she often answers: "Find something you love and do it well." Ashanti is still a young woman, and only the future will tell where she goes from here. Clearly, though, she is taking her own advice. She is searching for the music and the life she loves most—and then she is giving it her all.

1970s Hip-hop begins in the Bronx, New York.

1980 Ashanti is born in Glen Cove, New York, on October 13.

1998 Decides to forgo college for music.

2000 Signs with Murder Inc.

2001 Sings backup with some of the biggest names in music.

2002 Appears on *American Dreams* and *Sabrina, the Teenage Witch*.

Ashanti is released and quickly goes to number one on the *Billboard* charts, and becomes the seventh-highest-selling album of the year.

Ashanti becomes Murder Inc.'s top-selling artist.

Becomes the second artist to have her first three chart entries in the top ten at the same time.

Publishes a book of poetry and essays, *Foolish/Unfoolish: Reflections on Love*.

Wins two Lady of Soul awards, one Teen Choice award, two MOBO awards, and eight *Billboard* Music awards.

Performs at the Neil Bogart Memorial Fund's Annual Tour for a Cure.

2003 Appears on *Buffy the Vampire Slayer*.

Performs in support of VH1's Save the Music Foundation.

Releases her second album, *Chapter II*.

Wins two American Music awards, two Soul Train awards, one Nickelodeon Kids award, and an NAACP Image award.

Receives five Grammy nominations; she wins one.

2003 The offices of Murder Inc. are raided by the FBI.

The word "Murder" is dropped from the company name.

2004 Appears in the Bollywood film *Bride and Prejudice*.

Concrete Rose is released, and Ashanti becomes The Inc.'s top-selling artist for the third straight year.

Performs at the "Battle of Hope" concert in Nigeria.

2005 Appears in the film *Coach Carter*.

Appears in the made-for-TV movie *The Muppets' Wizard of Oz*.

Conducts a hip-hop dance workshop to aid the Hurricane Relief Fund.

Irv Gotti is arrested on money-laundering charges; he is found not guilty.

A jury finds Ashanti guilty of breach of contract with an earlier company.

Participates in Fashion Rocks to benefit the victims of Hurricane Katrina.

Participates in the *Today Show*'s Annual Toy Drive.

2006 Appears in the film *John Tucker Must Die*.

Announces the launch of OPC Beauty Blend vitamins.

Files a lawsuit to stop sales of an album made when she was sixteen.

2007 Appears in the film *Resident Evil: Extinction*.

Discography

Solo Albums

2002 *Ashanti*
Foolish/Unfoolish: Reflections on Love (spoken)
2003 *Ashanti's Christmas*
Chapter II
7 Series Sampler: Ashanti
2004 *Concrete Rose*
Maximum Ashanti
2005 *Collectables by Ashanti*

Number-one Singles

2001 "Always on Time" (with Ja Rule)
2002 "Foolish"

Book

2002 *Foolish/Unfoolish: Reflections on Love*

Selected Television Appearances

2001 *Saturday Night Live*
2002 *American Dreams*
Diary. Ashanti: Princess of Her Domain
Sabrina, the Teenage Witch
The Tonight Show with Jay Leno
2003 *Buffy the Vampire Slayer*
Intimate Portrait: Ashanti
Punk'd
VH1 Divas Duets
When I was 17
2004 *Apollo at 70: A Hot Night in Harlem*
Ashanti: Custom Concert
VH1 Divas 2004
Live with Regis and Kelly
2005 *An All-Star Salute to Patti LaBelle: Live from Atlantis*
Las Vegas
The Muppets' Wizard of Oz
Last Call with Carson Daly
The Tonight Show with Jay Leno
Ellen: The Ellen DeGeneres Show
Live with Regis and Kelly
Total Request Live

Film

2004 *Bride & Prejudice*
2005 *Coach Carter*
2006 *John Tucker Must Die*
2007 *Resident Evil: Extinction*

Video

2003 *Hip Hop Uncensored Vol. 5: The Greatest Shows on Earth*
2004 *Ashanti: Princess of Hip Hop Soul*
      Princess of Hip Hop
2005 *Kermit: A Frog's Life*

Awards

2002 *Soul Train* Lady of Soul Awards: Best R&B Soul New Artist;
      Aretha Franklin Entertainer of the Year

      Teen Choice Awards: Choice Breakout Artist

      MOBO Awards: Best R&B Act; Best Hip Hop Act (with Ja Rule)

      Billboard Music Awards: Female Artist of the Year; Top New
      Pop Artist of the Year; Hot 100 Singles Artist of the Year;
      R&B/Hip-Hop Artist of the Year; R&B/Hip Hop Female
      Artist of the Year; New R&B/Hip-Hop Artist of the Year;
      R&B/Hip-Hop Single of the Year; R&B/Hip-Hop Singles
      Artist of the Year

2003 American Music Awards: Favorite New Artist in Pop/Rock;
      Favorite New Artist in Hip/Hop/R&B

      Grammy Awards: Best Contemporary R&B Album

      Soul Train Awards: Best R&B Soul Single, Female; Best R&B
      Soul Album, Female

      NAACP Image Awards: Outstanding New Artist

      Nickelodeon Kids Choice Awards: Best New Artist

2004 Do Something Brick Awards: "Do Something" Brick Awards

Books

Ashanti. *Foolish/Unfoolish: Reflections on Love.* New York: Hyperion, 2004.

Stacy-Dean, Kelly Kenyatta, and Natasha Lowery. *Alicia Keys, Ashanti, Beyonce, Destiny's Child, Jennifer Lopez &MYA: Divas of the New Millennium.* Phoenix, Ariz.: Amber Communications, 2005.

Torres, Jennifer. *Ashanti.* Hickessin, Del.: Mitchell Lane, 2005.

Magazines

"Hot New Female Singers on Music Scene." *Jet,* April 22, 2002.

Norment, Lynn. "Ashanti Takes Charge on Her Way to Superstardom." *Ebony,* March 1, 2003.

Taylor, Amina. "Princess Reigns: Her Label's Legal Strife Aside, Ashanti Is on Top Form." *Voice,* December 11, 2005.

Web Sites

Ashanti
www.allmusic.com/cg/amg.dll?p amg&sql Bhhogtq6z9u45

Ashanti
www.mtv.com/music/artist/Ashanti/artist.jhtml

Ashanti Daily
www.ashantidaily.com

Ashanti: This Is Me
www.ashantithisisme.com

accolades—expressions of high praise.

anonymity—the state of blending into a crowd and going unnoticed.

Bollywood—the film and music industry of India.

breached—failed to obey an obligation.

chauvinistic—characterized by an attitude of superiority to the opposite sex.

collaborative—achieved by working together or with others.

controversy—disagreement felt strongly by all concerned.

debut—the first of something.

demeanor—someone's behavior, manner, or appearance, especially as it reflects on character.

diva—a distinguished woman singer.

exploitative—making use of someone unfairly.

genre—a category into which an artistic work can be divided on the basis of form, style, or subject.

gold—signifying that a record has sold 500,000 copies.

gospel—highly emotional evangelical vocal music that originated among African American Christians in the southern United States.

mediocre—adequate but not very good.

melding—blending.

misogynistic—characterized by the hatred of women.

money-laundering—the practice of engaging in financial transactions in order to conceal the identity, source, or destination of money.

objectification—the practice of reducing someone who is complex and multifaceted to the status of a simple object.

platinum—music having sold one million copies as a single or two million as a record or CD.

renaissance—a rebirth or revival.

royalties—a percentage of the sales of a piece of music that is paid to the composer.

tutelage—instruction and guidance.

vocal register—the range of a voice.

Rosa Waters has a degree in creative writing, and has written for various publications. She has worked in an inner-city crisis center, so she knows firsthand some of the challenges urban youth face. Although she makes no claim to musical talent of her own, her husband is active in the music scene, and the interface between creativity and culture is one of her ongoing interests.

Picture Credits

page

2: Murder Inc./Zuma Press	**31:** KRT/Darla Khazei
8: KRT/Lionel Hahn	**33:** Splash News/Brian Prahl
11: KRT/Olivier Douliery	**34:** NMI/Michelle Feng
13: KRT/Nicolas Khayat	**37:** PRNewsFoto/NMI
14: KRT/Lionel Hahn/Nicolas Khayat	**38:** Reuters/Fred Prouser
16: KRT/NMI	**41:** Zuma Press/Nancy Kaszerman
19: Zuma Press/Glenn Weiner	**42:** Zuma Press/Bryan Smith
21: Murder Inc./NMI	**44:** Zuma Press/NMI
22: Murder Inc./NMI	**47:** Paramount Pictures/NMI
24: PRNewsFoto/NMI	**48:** INFGoff/infusny-18
26: Zuma Press/Nancy Kaszerman	**50:** Splash News/Gregg Snodgrass
27: Zuma Press/Nancy Kaszerman	**53:** KRT/Giulio Marcocchi
29: NMI/Michelle Feng	**54:** Murder Inc./NMI

Front cover: Zuma Press/Paul Fenton-KRA
Back cover: UPI/Ezio Petersen